MW01229122

PROTECTING

PROVEN INSIDER

YOUR

INSURANCE SECRETS

VETERINARY

EVERY VETERINARIAN MUST KNOW

PRACTICE

BILL BUTLER

www.ButlerVetInsurance.com

Although the author has made every effort to ensure that the information in this book was correct at the time of first publication, the author does not assume and hereby disclaims any liability to any party for any loss, damage, or disruption caused by errors or omissions, whether such errors or omissions result from negligence, accident, or any other cause.

INSURANCE DISCLAIMER With respect to the reliability, accuracy, timeliness, usefulness, adequacy, completeness, and/ or suitability of information provided in this book, Bill Butler & Butler & Associates Insurance Agency, Inc., its partners, associates, affiliates, consultants, and/or presenters make no warranties, guarantees, representations, or claims of any kind. This book does not preempt or take the place of the actual insurance proposals or contracts. Please consult your policy for specific terms, conditions and exclusions. In the event you should have a specific question concerning your insurance program, please your insurance carrier or agent for advice. Testimonials are not representative. This book and all products and services are for educational and informational purposes only. Use caution and see the advice of qualified insurance professionals.

Copyright © 2022 by Butler & Associates Insurance Agency, Inc. DBA Butler Vet Insurance

All rights reserved. No part of this book may be reproduced or transmitted in any form or by any means, electronic or mechanical, including photocopying, recording, or any information storage and retrieval system, without permission in writing from the author.

ISBN:–Hardcover 979-8-9858187-0-3

ISBN:–Paperback 979-8-9858187-1-0

eISBN:–Ebook 979-8-9858187-2-7

*This paper meets the requirements of ANSI/NISO Z39.48-1992 (Permanence of Paper)

Cover Design and Layout: Dawn Teagarden
Author Photographs: Val Westover

BILL BUTLER'S

PROTECTING YOUR VETERINARY PRACTICE

Insider Insurance Secrets Every Veterinarian Must Know!

Special **FREE** Bonus Gifts for You!!!

To help you Protect Your Practice, there are FREE BONUS RESOURCES for you at:

www.ButlerVetBook.com

WHAT OTHERS ARE SAYING ABOUT BILL BUTLER & BUTLER VET INSURANCE

"This is a MUST READ for EVERY Veterinary Practice Owner! Bill Butler has written a simple guide for helping you protect your business and his ideas will have a major, positive difference in your life! I HIGHLY recommend Bill's book! If you're looking for an insurance agent who comes from the heart, truly cares about people and will put your best interest first, then do yourself a favor and work with Bill today! You will be Grateful you did!"

— **James Malinchak,** Featured on ABCs Hit TV Show, "Secret Millionaire" (Viewed by 50 Million+ Worldwide) Authored 27 Books, Delivered 3,000+ Presentations & 2,000+ Business Consultations Best-Selling Author of *Millionaire Success Secrets* Founder, www.BigMoneySpeaker.com

"Bill Butler is a role model for other independent insurance agents when it comes to professionalism, responsiveness and caring"

—**Kevin Steiner,** CEO & President West Bend Mutual Insurance Company

"I know from my own experience coaching is the number one way for anybody to take things to the next level, Bill invested in coaching to help his team and his clients. This book is a product of that coaching."

—**Joe Theismann,** President JRT Associates, Inc.

"Butler Vet Insurance takes care of our business needs, so we can take care of our patients"

—**Dr. Heather Taylor,** Owner, Grand Avenue Veterinary Center

"Bill has been a part of the Minnesota Independent Insurance Agents Association as a member, an emerging leader, a legislative committee member, and now a trusted advisory agent owner. Bill has learned and advanced in his level of knowledge immensely over the past 18 years even during tough personal times. He is always striving to learn more to make his customers' lives more safe, sound and secure and is a valued member of the association."

—**April Goodin,** Director of Operations,
MN Independent Insurance Agents Association

"Bill and his team at Butler Vet Insurance are a huge asset to my practice. Over the past few years my business has grown, and I have always been able to rely on Bill to make sure my practice has the insurance it needs. Having a trusted insurance advisor like Bill is a must for every practice owner."

—**Dr. Sven Kohlmyer, DVM,** Owner Wayzata Pet Hospital

"Since joining the Minnesota Veterinary Medical Association as an Industry Partner Bill Butler has always been willing to help our Veterinarians when asked. We are grateful for Industry Partners like Bill and the support he has provided to MVMA over the years because it shows that he values everyone's success within the Minnesota Veterinary Community, this book is another example of that support."

—**Kelly Andrews, CAE,** Executive Director,
Minnesota Veterinary Medical Association

"I am so thankful to have Bill as my insurance agent and appreciate his integrity and expertise. I have peace of mind knowing I have the coverage I need and am protected. Bill understands the veterinary industry and the concerns veterinarians face."

—**Dr. Amy Haarstad, DVM, DACVD,** Practice Owner, Haarstad Veterinary Dermatology

"I have known Bill since 2014 and he is one of the best independent insurance agents in the industry. I have seen his growth as an agency owner and thought leader in the industry. The level of investment in himself is uncommon in the insurance industry and watching him take action to author this book has been impressive to watch."

—**Russ Castle,** President Insurance by Castle

"I met Bill at a veterinary association event. At the time I didn't give my insurance much thought, until my renewal came with a significant rate increase. He was able to help me save money and keep the same coverage"

—**Dr. Coral Riggs, DVM,** Owner of North Paws Veterinary Clinic

"Bill took the time to help us with the special needs of house call practice. He let us know where we were already getting good rates and where we could improve. When I was declined for disability insurance for a policy through an association, Bill found a way for me to obtain policies for me and my practice. I will continue to use Bill for my insurance needs because of his honesty, integrity, and knowledge that he is looking out for me."

— **Dr. Ann M. Fischer,** DVM, Practice Owner

"Bill Butler became my insurance agent in 2019. I was struggling to find coverage for my building and business that fit my needs as a veterinarian. After talking with him for 30 minutes, I knew he was far more knowledgeable of the veterinary industry than any other agent I had spoken to before. He was able to find me better property coverage for the building, negotiated a decrease in my worker's compensation insurance, and tailored my business insurance to fit the needs of a veterinary clinic. If I ever had a question or issue, he has always been there to help. I recently sold my practice and he worked with the new owner group to obtain the coverage they needed while still protecting the building which I still own. I have recommended Bill to all of my colleagues who need veterinary business insurance, as I know he will take great care of them."

—**Dr. Jami Stromberg,** Doctor of Veterinary Medicine

"One of the most important decisions business owners make, but often take for granted, is who we are going to select to protect our greatest asset. It is my privilege to recommend the preeminent authority to protect your veterinary practice-Bill Butler and his team. Bill is the nationally recognized authority for the vet insurance industry, a speaker, author and a business leader. This book is revolutionary and reiterates why every veterinary practice owner must work with Butler Vet Insurance."

—**Mike Stromsoe,** Insurance Agency Owner, Author, Speaker, Business Coach, The Unstoppable Profit Producer

"I was first introduced to Bill Butler during a VHA webinar on Worker's Compensation insurance. I have been a veterinary practice owner for over 15 years but did not have a good understanding of our insurance policies, especially Worker's Compensation. Bill's presentation was well-organized and provided me with a much better understanding. I invited him to do a full insurance review for my practice, and after a thorough discussion of my individual needs we switched all of our policies over to Butler Vet Insurance. I highly recommend Bill Butler and Butler Vet Insurance for all of your veterinary practice insurance needs!"

—**Jennifer Blair,** DVM, CVA, CVFT, CTPEP, Hospital Administrator, Practice Owner, St Francis Animal Hospital / St Francis Integrative Services

"Bill's detailed knowledge of the veterinary field is evident, and is so valuable when it comes to insurance. We have also been impressed with his quick and thorough communication."

—**Dr. Leah Renne,** DVM

A colleague recommended Bill Butler and Butler Vet Insurance and I am glad they did. Bill was able to fill some gaps in coverage and make sure my practice is insured properly.

—**Dr. Rick Cameron,** Bass Lake Pet Hospital

MOTIVATE AND INSPIRE OTHERS!

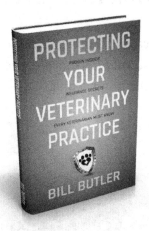

"Share This Book"
Retail $15.97

5–20 Books	$13.97
21–99 Books	$11.97
100–499 Books	$9.97
500–999 Books	$7.97
1,000+ Books	$5.97

TO PLACE AN ORDER CONTACT:

Butler Vet Insurance
Po Box 240326
Apple Valley MN 55124

Direct / Text 952-208-7220
Toll Free 800-750-9775

www.ButlerVetBook.com/Order

THE IDEAL PROFESSIONAL SPEAKER FOR YOUR NEXT EVENT!

Any organization that wants to educate their people on insider insurance secrets for Veterinary Practices needs to hire Bill Butler for a keynote and/or workshop training!

TO CONTACT OR BOOK BILL TO SPEAK:

Butler Vet Insurance
Po Box 240326
Apple Valley MN 55124

Direct / Text 952-208-7220
Toll Free 800-750-9775

www.billbutlerspeaker.com

THE IDEAL INSURANCE AGENT FOR YOU!

If you're ready to work with an agency and insurance professional that understands you and your industry you will love having Bill as your Agent!

TO CONTACT BILL BUTLER CIC, CISR, CWCA:

Butler Vet Insurance
Po Box 240326
Apple Valley MN 55124

Direct / Text 952-208-7220
Toll Free 800-750-9775

www.ButlerVetInsurance.com

For Mom, Dad, and my wife, Shannon.

CONTENTS

FOREWORD

Why *Protecting Your Veterinary Practice* Is a MUST Read

When Bill Butler let me know he was publishing a book to help veterinarian practice owners properly protect their practice by delivering preeminent insurance protection through the program he built, I was over-the-moon excited. Not for Bill, but for veterinary practice owners everywhere. Bill Butler is uniquely positioned to understand veterinary practices like no one else. Not only is Bill a business owner himself, but Bill is a lifelong animal lover and understands that every business owner invests a 100 percent unrivaled heart and soul commitment to their business every single day. Your business, to an extent, consumes your mindset daily.

This book will help thousands of people. Not only those who own and serve others in their veterinary practices, but the multitudes who are clients, family members, and friends of the people caring for the animals that are such a significant part of so many people's lives.

Bill Butler is a master at what he does. I vividly remember the first time I met Bill at a professional development event. I knew there was something different about him. Bill immediately started asking excellent questions, all surrounding becoming a better and more impactful agency entrepreneur. Having witnessed

Bill's phenomenal industry and personal development over many years, it's no surprise that Bill and his team have risen to the top as an insurance industry leader in protecting veterinary practices. Bill and his team keenly understand that veterinarians start their practices to care for animals but quickly find out that there is so much more to running their business, and their insurance program is just one piece of a confusing puzzle that can be costly and potentially devastating if done wrong. Bill wisely identified there was a gap for veterinarians and practice managers when it came to their insurance program for both coverage and service. This is the reason Butler Vet Insurance was created and I, personally, am so thankful Bill created this one-of-a-kind insurance program.

In this book, author, speaker, entrepreneur, and insurance agent, Bill Butler, shares his insider insurance secrets learned in the trenches to explain why unique insurance products and services are needed to protect veterinary practices in easytounderstand terms and concepts that will simplify insurance and provide a blueprint and action plan for protecting your practice.

It is an honor and a privilege to continue to learn from Bill Butler and witness his massive impact for the benefit of the veterinary industry. I am proud to introduce you to Mr. Bill Butler of Butler Vet Insurance, the author of this transformational book, *Protecting Your Veterinary Practice: Proven Insider Insurance Secrets Every Veterinarian Must Know*.

If you have any questions about Bill Butler, don't hesitate to contact me.

—**Mike Stromsoe,** Author, Speaker, Thirty-Five-Year Insurance Agency Principle, mike@upplife.com

Butler Vet Insurance

Protect Your Practice Blueprint

- Business General Liability
- Business Property
- Professional Liability Insurance
- Work Comp
- Cyber Liability
- Business Auto
- Life & Disability
- Employment Practice Liability

CHAPTER 1

HOW TO FIND THE RIGHT INSURANCE AGENT

There are many options when it comes to working with an insurance agent or agency to provide you with insurance products and services for your veterinary practice. Some of these are agents who represent only one insurance carrier, associations, your personal insurance agent, the agent who handled the insurance prior to you purchasing the practice, or the agent up the street. Any of these options can potentially work for you, but the question is how do you know if you are working with an agent that is right for you and your practice?

In today's world of "naming your price" and saving money by trying to do insurance fast and cheap, the insurance industry has commoditized itself. You should view your insurance agent as a trusted advisor on your intellectual board of directors, like your CPA or attorney. By valuing the relationship, you have with your insurance agent as a trusted advisor, it changes the relationship. The key for you is to make sure you are working with an insurance agent that knows your industry and understands the insurance needs of your practice.

In this chapter, I will give you the nine questions to ask every insurance agent you choose to do business with. By answering these questions, you will know if you have the right relationship with the insurance professional you use to protect your practice. The questions below are written as you should ask them to the agent or agency you are working with.

NINE QUESTIONS YOU SHOULD ASK
EVERY INSURANCE AGENT

One: Are You a Fully Licensed Agency?

By working with an insurance agency that has all of its insurance staff licensed in the states they operate in, you will receive a higher level of service. Unlicensed insurance agency staff cannot answer coverage questions, offer insurance advice, or discuss your policy with you. This can slow down your customer service requests and delay you in getting your questions answered. Only a licensed insurance agent can truly assist you with your insurance needs, as an unlicensed staff will fall into more of a processor role and in most cases will only be able to take a message and have licensed agents contact you back to answer your questions.

An insurance agency that licenses all of the sales and service staff places a high value on insurance education by making an investment in their team. This shows a higher level of professionalism within the insurance industry. In many cases, these agencies also send their agents to higher levels of continuing education and their team members attain designations within the insurance industry, just like the veterinary community. Designations within insurance show a higher level of knowledge of the insurance products and services offered by an agent or agency. It does not mean that agents without insurance designations are not good at what they do, but agents with insurance designations and agencies that invest in their team to acquire them generally take a coverage-first approach in working with their prospects and clients versus selling only based on price and trying to close a sale.

Two: Do You Represent Multiple Insurance Companies to Shop the Entire Marketplace to Find the Best Protection and Value for My Insurance Budget?

According to the Independent Insurance Agents & Brokers Association Market Share Report in their 2021 report (IIABA 2021) 86 percent of all commercial line premiums are written by Independent Insurance Companies. Historically, Independent Insurance Agents & Brokers have sold the majority of commercial insurance and that trend will continue into the future. The reason for this is Independent Insurance Agents & Brokers have access to many different carriers and coverage options. Direct writers or captive agents can place insurance with only one insurance carrier, and this limits the pricing and coverage options they can offer you.

By working with an Independent Insurance Agent or Broker your insurance program can be customized by placing your policies with different carriers to maximize your coverage and a better value in many cases. Oftentimes, the coverage offered is more specialized to a specific industry as well. At the time of writing of this book, just about all of the big-name national and regional insurance carriers have special policies designed for companion animal clinics. There are also special programs for mobile and mixed practices as well due to the unique nature of these types of veterinary clinics.

A direct writer or captive insurance may be able to assist you with your insurance needs, but you will have better-priced options with more coverage available through an agency that has more than one carrier option available to them.

Three: Do You Have Programs Specifically Designed to Protect My Practice?

Any insurance agency that is licensed to sell property and casualty insurance should be able to offer you a basic insurance policy for your practice. However, working with an agency or agent that has created a special program for veterinarians, like you, may offer special pricing and coverage tailored specifically to the needs of your practice. Usually, an insurance agency that has a "titled" program has taken the time to research the marketplace and put together a suite of coverages at preferred pricing for their clients. For example, at Butler Vet Insurance, we offer our Vet Pak Insurance Program where we custom design an insurance program within our Protect Your Practice Blueprint for the practices we work with.

Four: How Often Will I Hear from You? Will I Receive Ongoing Communication from Your Office?

When I meet with veterinarians, one of the biggest complaints I get is that they never hear from their agent or agency. The other issue is they don't even know who their agent is. As a commercial insurance client, you should be receiving timely and relevant communication from your agent regarding your insurance program. These could be things like, how to request certificates of insurance, update your payroll for workers' compensation, or request information prior to renewal. Other types of communication could include tips on reducing claims, recovery at work programs for injured employees, and more. Timely relevant communication is what you should be receiving from your agent or agency.

Five: Have You Fully Explained All of My Coverages to Me?
This does not only apply when you purchase your insurance or at an annual review, this should also happen at your first meeting with an agent. We review the existing policies and explain the coverages that are currently in place for a prospective veterinary client at our initial meeting. If there is an immediate insurance issue that needs to be addressed right away, it should be communicated during the initial meeting. A review and explanation of your existing policy prior to getting a proposal is always a good idea because that will show the agent's competency with your current policy.

While there is a time commitment in having your coverages explained to you, doing that up front can save headaches down the road. Later in the relationship, you only need to check in and update as needed or on an annual basis. Having a full explanation and conversation about your coverage allows you to ask questions and gain an understanding of your insurance policy and coverages.

During that initial meeting, coming prepared with a list of questions or concerns about the unique aspects of your practice is a good idea. Some of these may be what wakes you up in a cold sweat at two in the morning. What is the biggest headache or stress when it comes to your insurance program and finally, what isn't covered? What other insurance should we be investigating or looking to purchase? Agents should welcome these hard questions you ask as it relates to your insurance coverage and not try to hide or deflect their answers. Explaining how your current policy or the one they are offering to you will protect you when you need it the most—or more importantly how it won't—should be your agent's time to shine.

Six: Are There Easy, Flexible Payment Plans Available?

There are many newer billing options available with most insurance carriers. A large number of veterinary practices use large payroll services that also handle their workers' compensation insurance as well with the promise of easier billing tied to your payroll. These billing options are available through agents that represent the workers' compensation carriers, who provide these policies to the large payroll providers as well. Most practices we work with opt for the automatic billing options, though some just pay their premiums in full and many options in between.

Some policies may be billed through your insurance agency instead of directly to the insurance company and these are called agency-billed policies. This type of billing arrangement is usually in place for policies written through a special relationship that the agent or agency has to place the policy through a broker. These policies most often require the full annual premium when the policy is issued or renewed. If the agency billed premium amount is more than you prefer to pay all at one time, you can have the policy paid by a third party and you pay them back in installments; this is called Premium Financing. This allows you to go into a monthly billing plan and they bill you using installments and charge a small finance charge to loan you the money. These types of arrangements are quite common for larger agency-billed insurance policies.

Seven: Are You a Generalist or Do You Specialize in My Industry and Understand the Unique Risks of Insuring a Veterinary Practice Like Mine?

For agents in the insurance industry, you are considered a "generalist" if you write any type of business meaning, you will sell insurance to any type of prospect who calls your office. Almost all insurance agencies start as generalists, but some agents along the way gravitate toward a specific niche or industry. Some go into insuring long-haul trucking, craft breweries, pizza delivery, apartments, or, in my case, veterinarians. While there is nothing wrong with working with a generalist agent or agency, it is usually better to insure your practice with a specialist.

An insurance agency that specializes in working with veterinary clinics and hospitals is like a veterinary surgical specialist. They can offer a higher level of care because they have done it before. There is nothing wrong with working with a generalist but, as a medical professional, you know that a specialist in any field can be a much better option.

Eight: Are You Active in My Industry? Do You Belong to any Trade Associations?

An insurance agent or agency active in your industry and one that belongs to your associations is helping to support your industry and will have a better understanding of the unique needs of your practice. I belong to local and national associations within the veterinary industry, and it has been a fun bonus getting to support you and your industry as a business member. Veterinarians are good people who are fun to be around. We always look forward to our time at association conventions, expos, fundraisers, leadership summits, and social events. An insurance agency may write a number of veterinary practices but if they don't belong to the local or national associations that support your industry, ask them why they don't.

Nine: Is Your Service 100 Percent Guaranteed in Writing?

In the insurance industry, our product is a promise. A promise to provide our prospects and clients with insurance advice, products, and services that provide coverage when the worst happens. If we break that promise as an agent or agency, we should understand that we have lost your trust. That is why a satisfaction guarantee is something that should be offered to you. If at any point you aren't satisfied with the service, coverage, or relationship with your agent, you should be able to end the relationship and be refunded your unused premium, cancel your policy, and assist with your transition to another insurance agency, no questions asked.

If your current or future agent can't give you a guarantee in writing that they will do what they say they are going to do, how do you know they will have your back at claim time when there is a difficult billing issue, or provide the basic service that you deserve as a valued client of their agency? The answer to this question will tell you a lot about the future of business relationships with any agent or agency.

When you are looking to insure your practice, you are picking an insurance professional to help you with one of the most critical parts of your business and protect it when things go bad. Insurance agents get a bad rap for being slick or trying to sell cheap insurance which won't cover claims. I have been in the insurance industry long enough to know that, in many cases, we have earned our reputation. Armed with these nine questions, you can hire an agent that will work for you as a trusted advisor instead of just the person you pay for insurance.

IMPORTANT NOTE:

Any insurance professional should be able to answer these nine questions with no problem. If he or she cannot, it doesn't mean that they are not a good agent. It may mean that they are not up to the task of protecting you, your practice, employees, and everything you have worked so hard for.

ACTION ITEMS:

If it feels like you are being "sold" a policy instead of having a consultation, ask the nine questions above.

- If you currently have insurance in place, at your next renewal, ask your agent these nine questions to see how they answer.

- Find an independent niche specialist that works with veterinary practices.

- For insurance solutions that are best for your practice, contact me and I'll be happy to answer any questions you may have.

EMAIL: Bill@ButlerVetInsurance.com
PHONE 800-750-9775

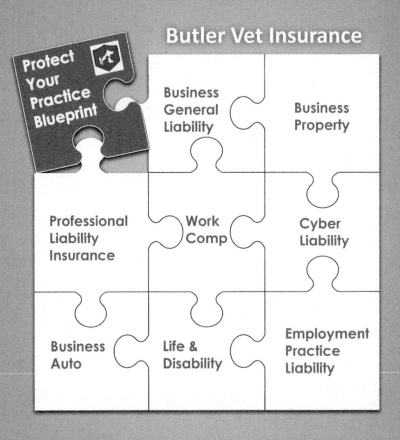

Butler Vet Insurance

Protect Your Practice Blueprint

Business General Liability

Business Property

Professional Liability Insurance

Work Comp

Cyber Liability

Business Auto

Life & Disability

Employment Practice Liability

CHAPTER 2

PROPERTY INSURANCE

Not having enough coverage for your building, practice equipment, medical supplies, and inventory can be a costly mistake but is easy to fix. Often when meeting with a veterinarian or practice manager, they don't know how much coverage they have, or who and why they picked their current level of coverage. If you are opening a practice, arriving at an amount of coverage is a little easier because you are purchasing all of your equipment, so you know how much you need to start. If you are a more established practice and have not kept up to date with reviewing your coverage or notified your agent when you added equipment or inventory, you most likely don't have enough coverage. This is the number one issue that comes up for the practices who opt to have a strategy session with me or my team.

With the increased cost of more advanced medical equipment such as digital X-rays, cold therapy lasers, and ultrasound, along with modern surgical and dental suites, it is easy to undervalue your equipment and not have enough coverage. Higher costs for building materials and labor also contribute to being underinsured for the cost to rebuild your practice, whether you rent or own. In this chapter, I will highlight the main coverages that we review with the practices we work with on an annual basis to make sure their largest financial investments are properly protected.

BUILDING COVERAGE

Most veterinary hospitals, clinics, and practices own their building either through the veterinary practice or in a separate corporation that owns it. In most cases, where the veterinary practice and building owner have common ownership, the insurance is placed through the veterinary practice insurance. Owning your building as a veterinary practice has many advantages and is usually one of the largest assets the practice has besides your revenue, which we will talk about in chapter 3.

In the world of commercial property insurance, your insurance carrier is only going to cover the cost to repair or rebuild the building. They don't cover the land or land improvements that you may have incurred when you built your building. Insurance to Value, or ITV, is the actual labor and materials cost that are needed if your building were in a total loss, like a fire or tornado. The Insurance to Value is calculated using software that is updated every few months or annually by insurance carriers to keep pace with the cost of labor and materials. Things like square footage, number of plumbing fixtures, stories, flooring, ceiling, and roof material, along with a list of other building options and items, are used in the calculation. Investing five minutes with your agent to verify the Insurance to Value on your building is accurate can prevent a huge gap in coverage. If it has been more than three years since you last reviewed your building coverage or purchased your policy from your current agent or agency, this should be reviewed to protect your biggest tangible asset.

There are many additional coverage options available to you based on the carrier who insures your building. If you are in an area that is coastal, flood, fire, or earthquake-prone, other coverages or policies may be needed because they may not be covered by your current policy. Make sure to ask your agent about these options depending on the location and state your practice is located.

If you don't own your building or are a tenant in a commercial building, like a strip mall, refer to the Leasehold Improvements section a little further in this chapter to make sure your investment in building out your location is properly protected.

Business Personal Property
This is all the "stuff" you have in your practice. If you run a traditional practice that doesn't have "mobile" operations, it is everything in your practice that isn't permanently attached to the building.

Your Business Personal Property, or BPP, would include things like:

- Medical/Surgical Tools
- Surgical Supplies
- Dental Equipment
- Diagnostic Equipment
- Lab Equipment & Supplies
- Office Equipment
- Desks, Chairs, Computers
- Office Supplies
- Leased Equipment
- X-Ray & Ultrasound
- *Special Consideration Should Be Given If You Have a CT or MRI
- Anything Not Permanently Attached...

The longer you have had your practice, the chances are you have added equipment over the years, so you need to carry more coverage. When I meet with prospective veterinary practices for strategy sessions and review their coverage, I ask the following question, "What would it cost to replace all of the equipment in your practice today if you had to buy it all new?" The answer often exceeds $500,000, and more commonly it's closer to $1 million. I have met with some practices that haven't updated their business personal property since they bought their practice and are underinsured by hundreds of thousands of dollars. During a recent meeting, the veterinarian who owned the practice told me they had just upgraded their older film X-ray to a brand-new digital X-ray, and when they called their agent to let them know about the equipment purchase, they were told to not worry about it, it was covered. This is how your practice ends up not having enough coverage when the worst happens.

When selecting an amount of business personal property coverage for your practice, you want to think about what it will cost to repair or replace everything in your practice at today's prices. You may have gotten a good deal on a used X-ray but if you needed to replace it at today's prices with a similar model, you are going to want to make sure you have adequate coverage.

LEASEHOLD IMPROVEMENTS

In the world of insurance, these are commonly called tenants improvements and betterments, or TIBs. These are your build-out costs in a building where you are the tenant and don't own the building. Sometimes these costs are listed as their own coverage or could be included in your business personal property. Make sure to account for your build-out costs on your policy either through tenants improvements and betterments coverage or business personal property coverage. Ask your agent what makes the most sense based on your insurance carrier and coverage needs. Sometimes insurance companies will offer either coverage, but one may be a lower premium than the other. Your agent should be able to advise you based on the insurance company you use, and your coverage needs.

ANIMAL BAILEE

Bailee coverage refers to other people's property that is in your care, custody, or control. Animal bailee coverage will provide protection for your practice in the event that one of your patients is injured or dies while under your care. This coverage can be added to some stand-alone professional liability insurance policies or your business owners' policy. When selecting a limit of coverage, you want to have enough to cover all your patients that may be lost in a single catastrophic event like a fire.

If you care for pure-bred companion animals, equine, bovine, or offer kennel and boarding as part of your operations, you should have higher limits of coverage. Lower limits, like $25,000 or less, usually don't require any additional documentation from the carrier but if you need higher limits of coverage, your insurance carrier may want to know the highest value of one animal or what the total would be if you lost all the animals under care in a single event, like a fire.

INLAND MARINE/SCHEDULED PROPERTY

This is special coverage that will provide a specific dollar amount of coverage for specific items. It is identical to your home insurance policy or scheduled personal property policy that provides coverage for a wedding ring or antiques. When you create an inland marine schedule, the items can be covered under a blanket or list the items individually. If listed individually, you will need to provide the following information: year, make, model, manufacturer, serial number, item description, value new, and/ or value to replace. If you are a mobile practice, you may need to insure your high-value practice equipment under an inland marine policy or scheduled property list to cover your business personal property off premises. If your practice offers any off-premises services, such as in-home euthanasia, you will want to confirm with your current agent that you have coverage for any of your medical or diagnostic equipment that leaves your practice.

COINSURANCE

Coinsurance is commonly used and often misunderstood in commercial insurance. It is an agreement between you and the insurance carrier that you will maintain a high enough percentage of coverage in exchange for having your claim fully covered by your insurance carrier. If there is coinsurance applied to your buildings or business personal property, it is listed on your declarations page as coinsurance 80 percent or coinsurance 90 percent next to the coverage it applies toward. What this means is that your insurance carrier is giving you the option of carrying less than the full value of the property, but it must be 80 percent or 90 percent of the full value to replace or repair the damaged property.

Your insurance carrier will not pay the full amount of the claim if you didn't maintain the proper amount of coverage as required by the coinsurance factor, which applies to the property insured. At the time a claim occurs, your insurance carrier will use the following formula to calculate if a coinsurance penalty applies.

VALUE OF COVERED PROPERTY (X) COINSURANCE

Limit of Insurance times (X) Total Amount of the loss less (-) Your Deductible

See the examples below.

Example #1 –Not Enough Insurance Coverage = Coinsurance Penalty

The value of the property is: $250,000

The coinsurance percentage is: 80%

The limit of insurance for it is: $100,000

The deductible is: $250

The amount of loss is: $40,000

Step (1) $250,000 x 80% = $200,000

(The minimum amount of insurance to meet your insurance requirements)

Step (2) $100,000 ÷ $200,000 = .50

Step (3) $40,000 x .50 = $20,000

Step (4) $20,000–$250 = $19,750

Your insurance carrier will pay no more than **$19,750.**

The remaining **$20,250** is not covered and you will need to rely on other insurance or absorb the loss yourself.

OUCH!

Example #2 –Adequately Insured = No Coinsurance Penalty

The value of the property is: $250,000

The coinsurance percentage is: 80%

The limit of insurance for it is: $200,000

The deductible is: $250

The amount of loss is: $40,000

Step (1) $250,000 x 80% = $200,000

(The minimum amount of insurance to meet your insurance requirements)

Step (2) $200,000 ÷ $200,000 = 1

Step (3) $40,000 x 1 = $40,000

Step (4) $40,000–$250 = $39,750

Coverage in example two is adequate, and no coinsurance penalty will apply. The carrier will pay the $40,000 loss minus the $250 deductible.

As you can see from the examples above, if you have coinsurance on your policy for your building or business personal property and you are not carrying an adequate amount of insurance, it could be very costly. Even a small claim could cost you thousands of dollars by not carrying the correct amount of coverage.

Coinsurance can be summed up like this: You should have carried a certain amount of coverage; but you didn't carry it, so the claim payout will be reduced according to the coinsurance penalty.

DEDUCTIBLES

Deductibles are pretty simple, they are your share of the loss. Deductibles can be represented in a flat dollar amount or a percentage of the coverage or claim. They generally only apply to property coverages but are sometimes present on Professional Liability policies, umbrella insurance, or other types of specialty policies. They can also be referred to as your self-insured retention, or SIR. An uncovered claim, or as we just discussed a coinsurance penalty, can also be considered a "deductible or self-insurance." Either the insurance carrier will pay for the claim or you are "self-insuring," which in the world of risk management means you are covering the claim personally and not through insurance.

In the case of flat deductible, if you have a large commercial building for your practice, carrying a higher deductible of $2,500 or $5,000 may save you some premium as your share of the claim is higher. I have seen practices with a $500 deductible on a building that is insured for over $1 million. They are asking the insurance carrier to pay a very high portion of any claim. The question you need to ask yourself in selecting the right deductible is what are you willing to pay out of pocket in the event of the claim? This can be driven by what you can afford, how much of the claim you are willing to take on yourself, and how much you would like to try and save on your premium. There is usually a point when increasing the deductible doesn't offer any additional savings and we discuss these options with the practices we work with.

Increasing your deductible can also offset the investment in adding additional coverages that may be missing from your current insurance program, such as employment practice liability or cyber insurance, which we will cover in later chapters.

ACTION ITEMS:

- Ask your agent if you have all the coverage needed based on the geographic location of your practice. If you are in a coastal, flood, fire, or earthquake-prone area, your policy may exclude these exposures, so ask about additional coverage.

- Do a mental or, better yet, a video/photo/itemized inventory to make sure you have enough coverage for all your business personal property.

- If you offer services away from your practice location, ask if you have enough coverage for your business property off-premises (equipment that leaves your practice).

- If you have coinsurance on your policy, verify that your coverage limits are accurate to avoid a coinsurance penalty.

- Ask your agent what deductible is right for you and your practice based on how much of a claim you want to pay and what you can afford.

- Find an independent niche specialist that works with veterinary practices.

For insurance solutions that are best for your practice, contact me and I'll be happy to answer any questions you may have.

EMAIL: Bill@ButlerVetInsurance.com
PHONE 800-750-9775

Butler Vet Insurance

Protect Your Practice Blueprint

Business General Liability

Business Property

Professional Liability Insurance

Work Comp

Cyber Liability

Business Auto

Life & Disability

Employment Practice Liability

CHAPTER 3

LIABILITY INSURANCE

PROTECTING YOUR ASSETS

Liability insurance is one of the most important coverages on an insurance policy and the great news is that it is often the least expensive coverage to purchase. Commercial general liability insurance is broken down into different categories, as shown on your insurance declarations pages. While you may be able to purchase less than $1 million of liability insurance, we do not recommend or offer less than that to the practices we work with. Anyone can be sued at any time for any reason and liability insurance should not be coverage you take a shortcut on.

Standard Commercial General Liability Insurance or CGL

- Occurrence Limit: $1,000,000
- The most your insurance carrier will pay for any *one* claim during the policy term.
- Aggregate Limit: $2,000,000
- The most your insurance carrier will pay for *all* claims during the policy term.
- Products/Completed Operations: $2,000,000
- Protection from lawsuits arising from products you sell under your brand name or label or completed services that do not fall under medical care.
- Fire Damage Liability: $300,000
- Protection for a tenant's liability due to a fire at a rented premises.
- Medical Payments: $10,000

- Pays for medical expenses only small claims that may occur at your practice.

One of the added benefits of liability insurance is that it also provides legal defense costs in the event you are sued or accused of negligence. The four elements of negligence are the following:

- Duty-owed to prevent injury or accident
- Breach of that duty by you
- Proximate cause of loss (you caused it)
- Injury or damage suffered by the injured party

Sometimes an accident or injury is out of your control, sometimes you know about an issue that may cause an injury and don't address it and someone gets hurt. In either case, your commercial general liability insurance will protect you and your practice.

There are other parts of a commercial general liability insurance policy that may vary from carrier to carrier, but the key components outlined above are common to most commercial general liability insurance.

How Much Liability Insurance Do You Need?

When speaking with veterinarians and practice managers about how much liability insurance they need, the conversation always comes down to three things.

1. How much you need.
2. How much you can afford.
3. How much you are comfortable with.

The "need" part of the conversation is pretty straightforward. You want to protect the total assets of your practice. This will include things like value of the building, business personal property, business savings, and gross revenue. When you get sued in a commercial insurance setting, the settlement requests get very high very quickly because there are more assets in play, including revenues. It's not just what you have now that you need to protect, it is what you will have in the future that needs protection as well.

It is important to protect *all* of your business assets, including your gross revenues. This is what you stand to lose if you are sued, whether you are negligent or not.

Commercial Umbrella
If the coverage on the commercial general liability isn't enough to protect all of your assets, you can purchase a commercial umbrella policy. An umbrella policy, or excess liability insurance policy, comes in two different types and provides extra liability protection in $1 million increments. If you opt to purchase an umbrella policy, it will do as it says and offer coverage for not only your business, but it will provide an "umbrella" over all of your commercial exposures, like workers' compensation and commercial auto insurance. There will be coverage requirements that may need to be met, which may require increases on the underlying policies.

An added benefit of commercial umbrella insurance policies is they often include extra coverages that may not be part of your business insurance policy. The most common additional coverages are the following:

- Libel
- Slander
- False arrest
- Infringing on another's copyright

- Malicious prosecution
- Use of another's advertising idea
- Wrongful eviction, entry, or invasion of privacy

For most veterinary practices you can expect to pay $300–$500 per $1,000,000 of coverage. This is a great value when considering what you get for the premium, peace of mind. The revenues that most practices earn along with building valuations and business personal property means you have more to lose than the average main street businesses. While a small slip-and-fall claim in your parking lot or waiting room, might not seem like a big deal when it happens, if you get served with a lawsuit seeking damages that small slip and fall it will become a big deal very quickly. Protecting all of your business assets with the proper amount of Liability Insurance is always a good investment.

ACTION ITEMS:

- Decide on the following for your liability insurance:
  What You Need, How Much You Can Afford,
  and How Much You Are Comfortable With.

- Ask for an umbrella policy quote if you don't have
  one—Common limits are $1 million–$10 million.

- Give yourself peace of mind by protecting ALL of your
  business assets with enough liability insurance.

- Find an independent niche specialist that
  works with veterinary practices.

For insurance solutions that are best for your practice,
contact me and I'll be happy to answer any questions
you may have.

EMAIL: Bill@ButlerVetInsurance.com
PHONE 800-750-9775

Butler Vet Insurance

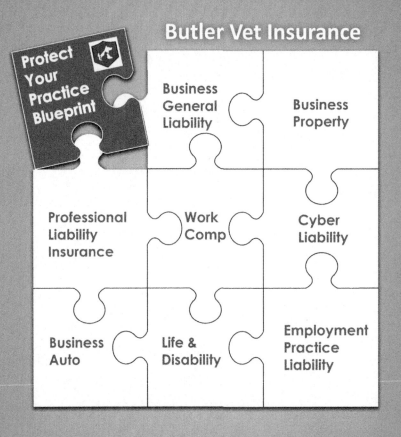

CHAPTER 4

WORKERS' COMPENSATION INSURANCE

Workers' Compensation insurance is required by law to pay for medical payments, lost wages, and other costs associated with an injury sustained on the job. At a veterinary clinic, regardless of your scope of practice, one thing is certain, you will have an injured employee, need to file a claim, and use your workers' compensation insurance. You may never file a property, general liability, or veterinary professional liability claim in your career, but you will need to file a workers' compensation claim if you have employees at your practice. In the insurance community, we use terms like frequency (how many claims are filed in a given time-period) and severity (how much the carrier pays out on a claim). Veterinary practices often have a high frequency but low severity. What this means for you and your practice is you will file a lot of claims over the course of owning your practice, but the payout on your claims will be relatively low. Contrast that with a steel mill where they may only file one work-comp claim a year, but the injuries that are sustained are much more catastrophic than a cat bite. This means a steel mill will have low frequency but very high severity.

Workers' compensation is generally 50 percent to 70 percent of the total premium paid by most practices in a given year due to higher payrolls for the size of your operations, the rate of remuneration (more on this later), and the fact that the insurance carriers know you will likely file a claim during the policy period. If your practice goes one or two years free of any injuries that require filing a claim you are running a safe practice and beating the odds. I have seen claims come across my desk for needle pricks that needed treatment and bloodwork for months, police K-9s attacking a vet tech during a routine visit, a CVT getting pushed into an exam table, hitting their head, causing a concussion and of course lots of small bites. The highest payout on a work-comp claim I ever had was from a practice manager slipping on an icy parking lot during a post office run, getting out of their car, and tearing their ACL, needing to have it surgically repaired. The point is, your practice is going to have workers' compensation claims and you are going to use your workers' compensation insurance.

In this chapter, I will explain workers' compensation insurance so you can better understand how the carriers come up with your premium, how you can control your work-comp insurance costs by managing claims when they occur, and how to make sure you complete your annual audit so that you aren't overcharged thousands of dollars.

WORKERS COMPENSATION PREMIUM

In my opinion, workers' compensation is one of the most straightforward and transparent of all insurance. You get to see behind the curtain, so to speak, and see exactly how your insurance carrier arrives at your annual premium is a simple math formula that all carriers use. I'll break it down for you here now.

Based on the occupation, or "classification," all of your employees are assigned a "class code" which is assigned a rate of remuneration. The rate of remuneration is the rate per $100 of payroll for a given class code. Every occupation has an assigned class code and a corresponding rate of remuneration. The most common class codes in the veterinary industry are listed below. Depending on your state, you may be able to assign individual class codes by occupation within your practice, or the State Workers' Compensation Insurance Association or Bureau will dictate which classification is used.

8844–Animal Hospital–Small Animal
8845–Animal Hospital–Small Animal
8831–Grooming–Boarding Kennel
8810–Clerical No Other Class

For example, if you are a companion animal practice, your carrier will assign class code 8844 Animal Hospital–Small Animal and a rate of remuneration of $1.12. For every $100 in payroll paid to your associates, techs, and receptionists, you owe $1.12 in unmodified workers' compensation premium. Workers' compensation policies are "auditable" policies, meaning the carrier checks to make sure what you told them you pay in payroll was accurate at the end of each policy term. You are asked to estimate what you think your payroll will be for a given insurance policy term and the carrier charges you based on your estimate, more on annual payroll audits later.

In the example below, let's use an estimated $500,000 of payroll/ remuneration under class code 8844.

Example

Payroll ÷ 100 X Rate or Remuneration = Unmodified Premium

CLASS CODE	PAYROLL	RATE PER $100	PREMIUM
8844–Small Animal	$500,000	$1.12	$5,600

Once your insurance carrier calculates your premium, there are rating factors applied for higher limits of insurance, experience modification if eligible, policy credits, or debits (discounts or surcharges), then the state compensation fund fees and taxes.

Workers' compensation is nothing more than a math equation based on your payrolls. Depending on the rules of your state, insurance carriers may charge a different rate per $100 of payroll for a given class code, and some carriers have multiple options as well. In Minnesota, where Butler Vet Insurance is headquartered, the rate of remuneration for 8844–Animal Hospital–Small Animal ranges from $0.79 to over $2.00 depending on your carrier. If your agent or agency does not keep a close eye on what you are paying per $100 of payroll or understand the workers' compensation marketplace for veterinarians, you could be overpaying thousands on your work-comp insurance for no reason other than your agent isn't reviewing your insurance policies. See the example below on what a $0.50 difference in the rate of remuneration makes on $500,000 in payroll.

EXAMPLE 1

CLASS CODE	PAYROLL	RATE PER $100	PREMIUM
8844–Small Animal	$500,000	$1.12	$5,600

EXAMPLE 2

CLASS CODE	PAYROLL	RATE PER $100	PREMIUM
8844–Small Animal	$500,000	$1.62	$8,100

Paying only $0.50 more per $100 of payroll your practice would be charged $3,500 more a year for workers' compensation insurance. In Minnesota, most veterinary practices are paying 22 percent more than they should for their work-comp insurance simply because their rate of remuneration is higher than it should be. For the practices I work with in Minnesota, this is one area where we are able to provide extra value.

A quick look at your work-comp policy to see what your practice is paying per $100 of payroll and working with an insurance agent or agency that understands your industry can save you thousands in just a few minutes depending on your state. In a state with a common class code and unified rate for all businesses in that class, there may be dividend programs available. Mixed, mobile, and large animal practices will pay more for their workers' compensation insurance because those class codes are charged a higher rate of remuneration based on the more serious injuries they could sustain. Below is an example of what rates a carrier would charge based on a given class code.

Classification Code	Rate of Remuneration
8844–Animal Hospital–Small Animal	$1.41
8845–Animal Hospital–Large Animal	$1.77
8831–Grooming/Boarding Kennel	$1.87
8810–Clerical–No Other Class	$0.15

Insurance carriers charge workers' compensation premium based on the likelihood an employee will be injured based on prior claims. As I mentioned earlier, you will file many claims over the course of owning your practice, the overwhelming majority will be minor and for less than $1,000, with no lost time from work for your employee. Contrast the rate per $100 a roofer pays. They don't have a lot of work-comp claims but when they do, they are really serious injuries.

Classification Code	Rate of Remuneration
5551- Roofing Contractor	$37.89

WORKERS COMPENSATION CLAIMS—THEY WILL HAPPEN

Claims are going to occur no matter how safe your practice is. A dog waking up from anesthesia and biting a CVT, or a simple cat bite from a feral cat, and you have yourself a claim. What you do next will often determine the outcome and final cost of the claim. If you have a larger practice with higher payrolls, this will affect your experience modification, which I'll address later in the chapter. If your practice is smaller, your carrier may assign a surcharge due to claims history. Claims will happen but what you do immediately after the claim can dictate how much the claim will cost in the end.

Sundown Rule

Institute a "Sundown" rule at your practice. Injuries may occur that don't require medical treatment but your leadership team at your practice needs to know about ALL injuries before the "sun goes down" on the day the injury occurs. This will allow you to take an incident report from the injured team member and any other team members who witnessed the incident. You don't want to find out on a Monday that you have a team member who can't come into work from an incident the prior Thursday. The faster you know about the injury and—if needed—file a claim, the lower the ultimate cost of the claim. Instituting a "sundown" rule at your practice allows you to manage the injury the same day it happens.

If you have a team member who needs medical care, that is of course the first priority. However, avoid the ER or urgent care if at all possible. Try to have minor injuries treated by the team member's primary care physician, which will keep the office visit costs down and avoid the ER visits, which are more costly. Most doctor offices hold open a few appointments every day for emergency visits, it may take longer for them to be treated that same day at their primary care doctor versus a trip to the ER, but it will keep the costs down of the claim. If it is a serious injury that needs immediate medical attention, a trip to the ER or urgent care is of course the best option. Another tip is if you have a higher number of claims due to the size of your practice, find a local doctors' office or clinic that you can send your injured team members to instead of the ER. This will save you time and money in the long run.

Incident Report

It is important to complete a first report of injury form for any and all injuries at your practice the day they occur. Your insurance carrier may provide one, there should be one specific for your state, or you can download one from our free resources website. Completing an injury report for every incident does a number of things for your practice. It shows your team members that you take their safety seriously, and you care about them and their well-being. Completing an incident report for all injuries, not just those that need a claim filed, also allows you to gather critical information on how injuries are occurring that you can review with your leadership team and discuss at your weekly or monthly staff/safety meetings. It has the added benefit of reducing the potential of insurance fraud because your team knows you get to the bottom of all injuries that occur at your practice. Even if a claim is never filed you have a record of who, what, when, where, and why an injury occurred, and if a team member comes back months later and says they are having issues related to an injury on the job you will have a record of the incident to file a claim.

Recovery at Work Program

One of the biggest mistakes that are made with workers' compensation claims is allowing injured employees to recover from their injury at home and not having them return to work as soon as possible. If the injured team member cannot perform their normal duties, you want to get them back working in any role they can perform based on the work restrictions as outlined by their medical provider. What most owners and practice managers often miss is that the wages paid as part of the work-comp claim count toward the total cost of the claim and can often be much more than the actual medical costs incurred. By having an injured team member back to work at the practice, even if it's only answering the phones or assisting with office work, it can reduce the cost of a workers' compensation claims by thousands of dollars. For more serious injuries and larger claims, if a team member is out more than eight weeks, the chance of them ever returning to their job goes down drastically. By creating a recovery at work program for your practice, you can reduce workers' compensation-claim costs which in turn can allow you to get the best pricing possible on your workers' compensation premium. There are tools and resources available to assist with creating a recovery at recovery at work program and we have some available on our free resource site to assist you.

Safety Plan & Meetings

The best way to manage claims is to prevent them from occurring in the first place. There are many resources out there to assist in creating safety plans, checklists, and procedures offered by insurance carriers, state, and national veterinary associations, including OSHA training. The hard work is getting something in place to start and assigning a key team member to manage your safety program and conduct your safety meetings. You can give them a leadership role within the practice and take the work off your hands as the owner or manager. By holding regular safety meetings, you can review a topic each month, have a local association provide training for your team, discuss any incidents that may have occurred and why it happened, and what your team can do to prevent them from happening in the future. Instead of looking at a monthly safety meeting as "work," use it as a team-building event to show your team you care about them and their safety while having some fun doing it.

PREPARING FOR YOUR ANNUAL PAYROLL AUDIT

A lot of focus on workers' compensation insurance is paid to injuries and claims, your annual payroll audit is where you will want to make sure you don't cut any corners. It is important you invest the time needed to prepare for your audit, and give complete, accurate, and clear information to the auditor so you can prevent being overcharged for an incorrect audit.

When you start your policy, you estimate your payroll at the beginning of each policy term, so you pay an "estimated premium." At the end of each policy term, your insurance carrier conducts a payroll audit and converts your "estimated" payroll to "actual" payroll, and recalculates the premium owed for the policy term. If you underestimated your payroll at the beginning of the policy year, you would owe the carrier premium and the premium is considered fully earned, meaning you will owe the full amount when it is billed to you. It is fully earned because it was for insurance coverage that occurred in the past and it is owed to the carrier because they would have covered a claim. With higher payroll, you have a higher chance of a claim and more premium you are required to pay as outlined earlier in the chapter based on your payroll and rate of remuneration.

Preparation for your annual workers' compensation payroll audit can make the process run smoothly and cut down on errors that will benefit the carrier and mean you pay more than you should.

Below are the steps for a smooth audit.

1. Assign a knowledgeable, friendly staff person to work with the auditor.

2. Treat the auditor as a welcomed guest—provide a clean, well-lit workspace if in person.

3. Present the auditor with your premium audit package, which should contain:

   a. Summary worksheet

   b. Copies of payroll report

   c. Copy of payroll tax returns (941, NYS-45-ATT, W-4-B)

   d. Copies of certificates of insurance

   e. Contracts with bills/invoices showing breakout of materials

   f. Cashbook/checkbook/general ledger

7. Offer no information unless the auditor asks for it.

8. Escort the auditor if they ask to tour facilities.

9. Schedule the audit for a Friday afternoon.

10. Wear appropriate attire:

    a. Clerical people in clerical attire, etc.

More often, payroll audits are being completed remotely, over the phone, or by submitting your audit to a portal. In either case, investing time preparing for your audit can prevent your practice from being overcharged on your workers' compensation insurance. Once the audit is complete, always request a copy of the auditor's worksheet, a copy of the final audit, and verify their worksheet matches your submitted payrolls.

Workers' compensation audit checklists, forms, and a preparation guide can be found online with our free resources.

Experience Modification and Your Practice
Over half of the practices I work with have never heard of or understood what their experience modification is and some have owned their practices for a decade or more. How experience modification is calculated, what your "mod" does to your premium, and how you can control your "mod" are all questions I'll cover in the rest of this chapter.

Experience modification or experience rating is a credit (discount) or debit (surcharge) based on your practice loss and payroll history over a given period of time. It is like a grade for your practice claims history against all other comparable practices. A mod of

1.00 would be graded a C, .80 would be given an A, and 1.20 is flunking and getting an F. An experience mod of .80 is a premium credit/discount of 20 percent and a mod of 1.20 is a premium debit/surcharge of 20 percent.

Not every practice is eligible for experience rating. Below are sample guidelines for receiving experience modification.

Your practice must be in business for at least two years and meet one of the following premium criteria:

- $12,500 of unmodified premium in the first year of the experience rating period.

- An average of $12,500 unmodified premium in the first two years of the experience rating period.

- If you have more than two years of experience, you must have an average annual unmodified premium of $6,250 in the experience rating period.

Unmodified premium is your practice payroll (remuneration) times the rate of remunerations (rate per $100 of payroll) charged by your insurance carrier. If you are not eligible for an experience rating, it will not show up on your declaration page or it will be represented by 1.00, which is called "unity." The jurisdiction you fall under will limit large claims in a given year to a dollar amount across all industries. This will vary from year to year.

Below are the elements that are used to calculate your experience modification.

Elements of the experience rating plan formula:

- ACTUAL LOSS = Total value of claim including reserves.

- PRIMARY LOSS = Reduced amount of
  claim used in the formula.

- EXPECTED LOSS = Amount of claim your business
  is expected to have based on your business
  type (class codes) and size (payroll).

Formula Factors:

- EXPECTED LOSS RATE = Factor used to determine the
  amount of losses by class code expected by the formula.

- D RATIO = Discounts the expected loss total
  to arrive at the expected primary loss.

- WEIGHT FACTOR = Percentage of actual
  losses used in the formula.

- BALLAST FACTOR = Stabilizing element that limits
  modification fluctuation in the formula.

Three years of payroll and claims data is used to compile your experience rating. Those three complete years of "experience" end one year prior to the effective date of experience rating.

EXAMPLE:
Rating period when you experience modification is
calculated–2021
Policy Periods used -
2020 skipped
2019, 2018, and 2017 payroll and claims data will
be included

What this means is that if you have a lot of small claims year after year, or one really bad claim every few years, it will be hard to have a more favorable experience modification and these claims stay with your mod for a number of years.

The good news is your practice has some control over your experience modification. Here are some tips for keeping your experience mod lower.

Tip #1: Medical-only claims are reduced by 70 percent—Have a recovery-at-work program.

What this means for you and your practice is if you have a team member with a cat bite that requires a doctor visit and antibiotics only, and they are back on the job the same day with no lost time, the claim amount will be reduced by 70 percent when it shows up on your experience modification worksheet. A $1,000 medical bill will only be shown and calculated as $300. That is why it is critical your team members do not miss any time from work.

When a team member misses any time from work due to an injury, the full medical payment will be used along with lost wages paid as part of the claim. This is shown as indemnity on a claim. So, using the $1,000 medical bill example from above the full amount of the medical payment will now be used in addition to the lost wages. If that team member is DVM, and they miss two weeks and are paid $3,500, the total amount of the claim is now $4,500 for the calculation of your experience modification instead of only $300 because they missed two weeks of work! It is critical to have a recovery-at-work program so you can have an injured team member back on the job as soon as possible with no lost time.

Tip #2: Make sure you don't have open claims with high reserves one hundred days prior to your work comp renewal.

When you file a claim, the insurance company the adjuster assigned to the claim assigns a "reserve" or the maximum amount your insurance company thinks a workers' compensation claim will cost them. If you have a team member bitten by a stray cat that needs a rabies vaccination, your insurance carrier may assign a $15,000 reserve to that claim. This amount is what shows up on your claim report and if it stays open for a long period of time and is not closed, $15,000 is what will be used in your mod calculation. If the claim is finally closed for $2,000, the remaining reserve of $13,000 will be removed.

You should be checking with your agent one hundred days prior to your renewal to close any open claims so the reserves can be removed and not affect your experience modification. Your experience modification is calculated sixty days prior to the renewal and, once calculated, it is hard to change. You can only change it with data submitted to the carrier and if you have open claims with a high reserve, it cannot be changed. Once a claim closes, your experience modification is not recalculated at that time because it is generally only calculated once a year. Any changes to a claim during the year are calculated the following year.

Tip #3: Try to reduce the number of claims your practice has.

One large claim for $10,000 may have less impact than ten claims that total to $10,000. Workers' compensation claims are going to occur at your practice, training your team, conducting safety meetings, collecting a loss report for each and every claim, along with reviewing why the injury occurred can help you reduce the number of claims that occur at your practice over time. Workers' compensation carriers may even give a discount for having a safety program and you should ask your agent about it.

Tip #4: Work with an insurance professional who understands your industry and Workers' compensation.

By working with an insurance professional who truly understands your profession, they make sure you are getting the best rate possible, your experience modification is the best it can be, and offer you tools and resources to lower your premiums.

Your experience modification is nothing to be scared of, it is the one part of a workers' compensation policy that you have the most control over by how you run your practice.

Workers' compensation insurance is most likely your largest property casualty insurance expense. It is calculated by the amount of payroll your practice has and the rate of remuneration. You can control many parts of this required insurance. With your building or business property, there are many factors that go into what premium you pay but, with workers' compensation, if you work with an agent that has the top carriers and experience working with a practice like yours, it will help a great deal. Additionally, if you run a safe practice and your team members don't miss time from work when injured, you will have control over your program and can make sure you aren't one of the many practices overpaying for your workers' compensation insurance.

ACTION ITEMS:

- Put in place a sundown rule for all injuries.

- Collect a first report of injury for all injuries.

- Create a recovery-at-work program.

- Create a safety plan, assign a team member to "own" the program, and hold a monthly safety meeting with your team.

- Create a payroll audit renewal checklist and train your team members that will handle your work-comp audits.

- Check your experience modification if eligible.

- If possible, get any open claims closed or reserved reduced one hundred days prior to your renewal.

- Find an independent niche specialist that works with veterinary practices.

For insurance solutions that are best for your practice, contact me and I'll be happy to answer any questions you may have.

EMAIL: Bill@ButlerVetInsurance.com
PHONE 800-750-9775

Butler Vet Insurance

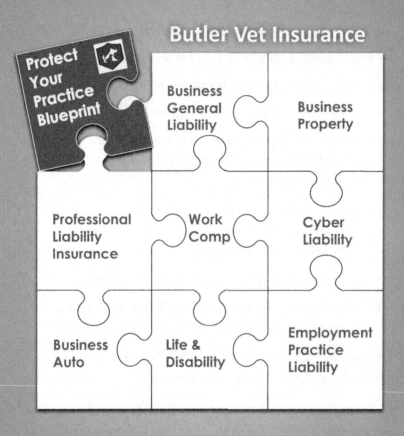

CHAPTER 5

COMMERCIAL AUTO

Commercial auto insurance for most veterinary practices is fairly simple but there are some items that your practice will want to make sure are addressed. First, do you need commercial auto insurance or a business auto policy (BAP)? The answer is yes, every practice should have some commercial auto insurance coverage even if your practice doesn't have a vehicle titled to the practice. First, I'll address personally owned versus commercially owned vehicles and why it matters.

PERSONALLY OWNED VEHICLES VS. COMMERCIALLY OWNED VEHICLES

The issue that comes up, usually toward the end of the year, is when a tax professional makes the recommendation to transfer the title of your family grocery getter over to the name of the practice. Once that occurs, you need to purchase a business auto policy and the reason for this is most personal insurance policies will not insure a vehicle owned by a corporation, even if you own the corporation.

Your personal auto policy is designed and rated by your personal auto insurance company with personal—not commercial—use in mind. You are being charged a premium based on personal use and not a commercial. Even if you are not a mobile practice or one that does house calls in the case of mixed or large animal practice, the claim amounts are much higher when a business is involved in the accident. With the practices we work with, $1 million is the starting point for coverage on any business auto policy coverages because you need to protect the assets of the practice. The practice needs protection in the event there is an incident with a personally owned vehicle, and I will address it in more detail.

The other big consideration is if you transfer the title of your personal vehicle over to the practice. Generally, only listed drivers may be covered. On almost all personal insurance policies, there is "permissive use," meaning you can loan your car to anyone to drive, and they have coverage under your insurance. Business auto policies with some insurance companies only listed drivers are covered and what this means for you is if you have a seventeen-year-old at home that may drive your commercially insured vehicle owned by the practice, they must be listed on the policy to be covered in the event of an accident. Many insurance carriers request a driver list every year.

When in doubt, have a conversation with your insurance agent or agency to understand the ramifications of transferring the title from a personally owned vehicle to the name of your practice before you make the change. While there may be tax advantages in transferring the title of your personal vehicle to your practice there will be insurance implications and increased insurance premiums associated with the change in ownership. Using your personal vehicle for business is not a problem as long as you aren't doing any sort of delivery and you have the vehicle insured for business use on your personal auto policy.

COMMERCIAL COVERAGE SYMBOLS EXPLAINED

So your practice owns a vehicle and you have a business auto policy. You are looking at your insurance policy and there are numbers in boxes for the type of coverage you have. These are called coverage symbols, and they explain what type of coverage you have for that specific vehicle. There are different costs for using different coverage symbols because some afford more coverage and some offer less coverage. Below outlines what each coverage symbol means and how coverage is applied. These are taken from the Insurance Services Office business auto coverage (Insurance Services Office 2013) form and may be different with your specific carrier.

1–Any Auto	Use for liability insurance only. Includes coverage for owned, non-owned, and hired autos. Provides automatic coverage for autos the insured newly acquires.
2–All Owned Autos	Applies only to autos owned by the insured, and for liability coverage on any non-owned trailers while attached to power units the insured owns. Provides automatic coverage for autos the insured newly acquires.
3–Owned Private Passenger Autos	Provides automatic coverage for private passenger autos the insured newly acquires. Use for liability, medical payments, uninsured and underinsured motorists, physical damage coverages, or towing.
4–Owned Autos Other Than Private Passenger	Provides automatic coverage for other than private passenger autos the insured newly acquires. Use for liability, medical payments, uninsured and underinsured motorists, and physical damage except towing.

5–All Owned Autos That Require No-Fault Coverage	Provides automatic coverage for autos the insured newly acquires where no-fault is required by law. Used only for P.I.P. and Additional P.I.P.
6–Owned Auto Subject to Compulsory Underinsured Motorist Law	Provides automatic coverage for autos the insured newly acquires where rejection of Underinsured Motorist is not permitted by law.
7–Autos Specified on Schedule	Applies only to those autos described on the schedule for which a premium charge is shown, and for liability coverage on any non-owned trailers while attached to power units the insured owns. Provides no automatic coverage for autos the insured newly acquires. The company must be notified of newly acquired autos within 30 days. *Used for all coverages.*
8–Hired Autos	Applies only to those autos leased, hired, rented, or borrowed by the insured. This does not include any auto leased, hired, rented, or borrowed from any of the insured's employees or members of their households.
9–Non-Owned Autos	Applies only to those autos not owned, leased, or hired by the insured that are used in connection with the insured's business.

Depending on the symbol selected for the specific coverage, you will be charged a different premium. The best example is symbol

1 versus symbol 2. Symbol 1 will provide you coverage for **ANY** vehicle you happen to be driving, even if you don't own it. Symbol 2 will only provide coverage to **OWNED** vehicles. With both of these coverages, you automatically have coverage afforded for newly purchased vehicles. Symbol 7 only provides coverage to those vehicles listed on the vehicle schedule.

Symbols 1 and 2 cost more because the insurance carrier needs to cover vehicles that you may drive or purchase without their knowledge but, in the case of Symbol 7, if it isn't listed then the insurance company doesn't have to cover the vehicle. Symbol 7 costs less on your business auto policy but you need to stay current with your vehicle schedule. These symbols are set up when you purchase your commercial insurance policy and you should consult with your agent or agency to make sure you have the right symbols based on your coverage and insurance budget needs.

HIRED AND NON-OWNED AUTO COVERAGE

If you, your practice manager, associates, or any team members use their privately owned vehicles in the course of their employment, you need hired and non-owned coverage. Every practice should carry hired and non-owned auto coverage, even if your practice doesn't own any commercial vehicles. This inexpensive coverage will help pay a claim for rented, borrowed, or hired vehicles, or a claim against your practice for a work-related car accident in a personally owned car.

Hired Auto Coverage

This coverage refers to coverage for "hired autos" that your practice may rent, hire, or borrow. If you travel to an out-of-state convention and rent a car with your company credit card this would be considered a "hired auto." If you, your practice manager, or another team member are involved in a car accident when driving a hired, rented, or borrowed vehicle in the course of business, this coverage will help pay for the liability costs.

Non-Owned Auto Coverage

If you don't own, lease, or hire a vehicle and your employees use their own vehicles for business activities for the practice, those are non-owned autos. This is the practice manager making a run for office supplies or trips to the bank or post office. If you or that team member are involved in a car accident in a personally insured vehicle, this coverage would pay for a claim brought against the practice. The personal auto insurance policy would provide coverage to the employee for the accident, but the practice also needs protection in the event it is brought in on the claim.

These coverages can be added to your business auto policy, or can be endorsed onto your business owners policy and is relatively inexpensive.

ACTION ITEMS:

- Confirm you have hired and non-owned auto coverage on your practice policy, or BAP (make sure you are only buying it on one policy).

- Check with your insurance agent before transferring your personal vehicle title to your practice on any potential issues.

- Verify the coverage symbols are appropriate for your practice if you have a commercially owned vehicle.

- Find an independent niche specialist that works with veterinary practices.

For insurance solutions that are best for your practice, contact me and I'll be happy to answer any questions you may have.

EMAIL: Bill@ButlerVetInsurance.com
PHONE 800-750-9775

Butler Vet Insurance

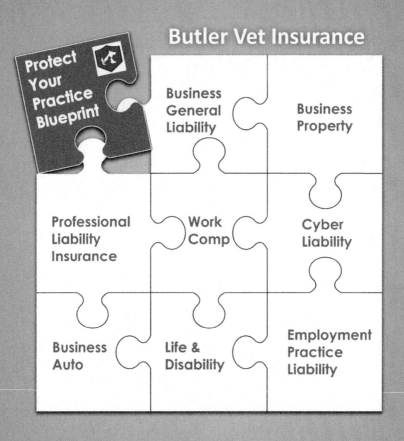

CHAPTER 6

EMPLOYMENT PRACTICE LIABILITY INSURANCE

Employee-driven lawsuits are unfortunately becoming more common and can be very costly to your practice. Here are some startling statistics from TrustedChoice.com.

- Over the last twenty years, employee lawsuits have risen roughly 400 percent, with wrongful termination suits jumping up more than 260 percent.

- Roughly 41.5 percent of employee lawsuits are brought against private companies with less than one hundred employees.

- The cost of settling out of court averages $75,000, and the average court settlement fee is $217,000 if you lose the case.

- Businesses are three times more likely to be sued by an employee than experience a fire.

- The average cost of employment liability lawsuits rose 26 percent in the last three years.

- Six to ten businesses that don't buy employment practice liability insurance mistakenly think they have coverage under other policies.

- Seven out of ten businesses don't carry employment practice liability insurance.

As you can see from the startling facts above, protecting yourself from an employee-driven lawsuit is an important part of protecting your practice. Below are examples of employee-driven claims that could be covered by employment practice liability insurance.

- Sexual harassment

- Wrongful termination
- Breach of an employment contract
- Discrimination
- Negligent HR decisions
- Inaccurate employee evaluations
- Violation of local and federal employment laws
- Infliction of emotional distress or mental anguish
- Failure to employ or promote
- Wrongful discipline or demotion
- Mismanagement of employee benefits
- Defamation of character
- Privacy violations

Because of the unique business operations associated with a veterinary practice, employment practice liability insurance is harder to purchase than most other businesses. You fall under the medical office classification and those are traditionally hard to insure for employment practice liability due to the emotional and mental aspect of working at a veterinary practice or medical office. It is critical to purchase this coverage as part of your insurance program.

Why else should you buy this employment practice liability insurance? If the claim or lawsuit is baseless, your employment practice liability policy will pay your legal defense costs which, in many settlement cases, are a larger share of the overall cost of the claim. Lawsuits for discrimination and harassment are more common and carrying enough coverage is more important than ever. This is valuable coverage in a couple of different ways. The first is to add it to your business insurance policy, which is a fast and easy way to purchase some protection against the claims listed earlier. The second and best way to protect your practice is to purchase a stand-alone employment practice liability policy, which will offer more coverage and sometimes coverage for events that happened prior to even purchasing the policy and also covers acts by third parties. Either way, having some protection for employee-driven lawsuits is critical to your insurance program and protecting your practice.

Very early on in my insurance carrier, I was working with some new business owners. They had the option to add some employment practice liability protection at a very reasonable price relative to the number of employees they had on their team. For two years in a row, they decided not to add the insurance, and when I pressed them on the importance of protecting their growing business, they gave the answer I get all the time, "We don't need that here, every one of our team members is like family." Just a few months later, when they were in the middle of opening another location for their business, the owner was accused of sexual harassment and intimidation.

When I received the call from my clients requesting a meeting to discuss the claim, I knew it was going to be a very difficult meeting. The first question my clients asked was, "Was this the coverage we declined the last couple of years?" I had to say yes, it was, I then told them the three words you never want to hear from your insurance agent, *"It's not covered."* The claim, with legal fees, was over $80,000. They could have had coverage for less than $3,500 a year, saving their business over $75,000.

Please take the time to research purchasing employment practice liability insurance from your insurance agent or agency; it is important to the long-term success of your practice.

ACTION ITEMS:

- Check with your agent or agency to make sure you have employment practice liability insurance.

- Ask if your policy covers prior acts and offers third-party coverage.

- Ask if your policy provides defense outside of your policy limits.

- Discuss what level of protection is right for your practice, based on the number of team members and business assets.

- Find an independent niche specialist that works with veterinary practices.

For insurance solutions that are best for your practice, contact me and I'll be happy to answer any questions you may have.

EMAIL: Bill@ButlerVetInsurance.com
PHONE 800-750-9775

Butler Vet Insurance

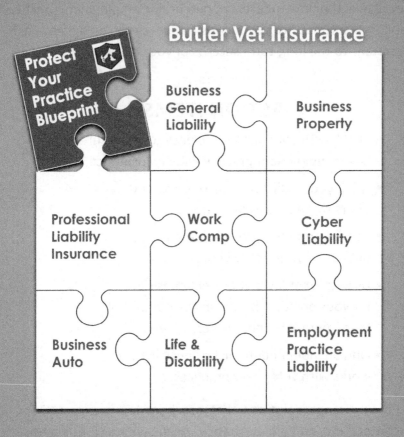

CHAPTER 7

CYBER LIABILITY INSURANCE

Cyberattacks on small businesses are now the norm and veterinary practices are not immune. In fact, you are more at risk than most other businesses. Gone are the days when cybercriminals only targeted large corporations for their data to sell on the dark web. Now, main street businesses like your practice are targeted along with multinational corporations, but you don't have the large-dedicated teams of IT professionals to help you navigate protecting your practice. Now, we are a society that depends on "the Cloud," use technology in every aspect of daily life, and even if your practice still maintains paper files, chances are you have a connected device in your clinic that relies on the internet like your copy machine, lab equipment, or digital x-ray.

Front-end protection is critical for your practice because the medical profession as a whole is one of the most targeted groups in the business community due to the type of large volumes of information that is collected and stored. While you store very little information on your pet owners that would be targeted in a cyberattack, the fact that most modern veterinary practices rely heavily on cloud-based services for your patient file management make you prime targets. I know of a case where a veterinary practice was targeted by mistake because the cybercriminals mistook them for the local human hospital in their small town.

Hacking, ransomware, social engineering, phishing, malware, Trojan horse, and bricking are now common occurrences for small businesses and veterinary practices. This is a fast-moving risk to society as a whole for the government, IT community, and the insurance industry, and we are all having a hard time keeping up with the cybercriminals. Right now, everything we are doing is from a risk mitigation standpoint and is very reactionary.

When I started my insurance career in 2004, cyber risk insurance was only sold to the biggest of corporations and there were very few places to purchase a cyber insurance policy for most main street businesses like your veterinary practices. Back then, you could add some coverage onto your business owner's insurance policy that would give you $50,000 or $100,000 in data breach coverage and that may be enough to cover the claim. Now, there are hundreds of carriers offering coverage with just as many coverage options in a cat-and-mouse game with cybercriminals.

CYBER CRIME

It used to be that you needed to be a sophisticated computer hacker to hack into companies and steal their data. Now, however, you only need a few hundred dollars and access to the Dark Web to purchase the code needed to bypass a company's IT defenses along with buying a million emails or so to send it to. Cybercriminals can now go online for the tools they need to steal and extort a business like they are shopping on Amazon. They are evolving almost daily in how they target businesses and your data.

The Ponemon Institute recently reported that 50 percent of small- and medium-sized US businesses had suffered a data breach, with 55 percent suffering a cyber-attack. The most common attack is non-sophisticated phishing attempts.

Below are some of the most common types of cyberattacks.

Malware

Malware is a broad term used to describe a large number of cyberattacks like viruses, Trojan horses, worms, and spyware. These types of attacks generally install malicious programs or software onto your computer system. They most commonly come in the form of links or attachments on emails or websites. Below are common types of malware.

- **Viruses**—Viruses infect your system and attach to applications' initialization sequences. They can replicate and create an .exe extension that is a virus file that mirrors the real one.

- **Trojan Horse**—Malicious software hidden inside a useful program that once loaded onto your system is used as a back door for cybercriminals to steal data or other illegal activities.

- **Worms**—Worms are often installed through email attachments, sending a copy of themselves to every contact in your email list. These can overload your email server and cause a denial-of-service attack.

- **Ransomware or Cyber Extortion**—a type of malware that denies access to your data, threatening to publish or delete your information or data unless you pay a ransom. Other ransomware attacks use crypto-viral extortion, encrypting your information unless you pay the ransom and receive the description key.

- **Spyware**—a program that collects information about you and your computer usage. The cybercriminal can then install other malware, steal passwords, banking information, or commit a ransomware attack.

Distributed Denial of Service

A denial-of-service attack will flood your system with information or traffic overloading the system and crashing it. What these do is crash your system and deny the ability to respond or take the system offline completely.

Bricking

This type of attack is often associated with a ransomware or cyber extortion attack. If you don't pay the ransom, the cyber attacker will damage your computer or device to the point where it will no longer work properly, effectively turning your computer into a "brick."

Password Attack

Passwords are the most widespread method of protecting your information across technology platforms which makes them a prime target for cybercriminals. Passwords are a very attractive target for cyber attackers. There are a number of ways that a cybercriminal may try to use a password to gain access to your systems, such as social engineering or brute force attacks.

Social Engineering

This is the practice of manipulating someone into divulging information or passwords by clicking on links or paying phony invoices, and tricking you into providing otherwise confidential information to cyber attackers or third parties.

Cryptojacking

This type of cyberattack hijacks your computer for the purpose of mining cryptocurrencies. The attacker places software on your systems so they can use it to mine for cryptocurrency without your knowledge.

Spam or Phishing

One of the most common types of cyberattacks involves sending a large number of emails that appear to come from you or other trusted sources. The emails are disguised to look like legitimate emails but will contain viruses, malware, or links to websites that contain code to infect the receiver's computer. These can take place on social media sites, texts, or emails. Social engineering plays a huge role in the ability of cybercriminals to use spam or phishing to get unsuspecting recipients to click or open infected emails, texts, attachments, or links. There are several different types of phishing attacks, including:

- Spear Phishing—Targeted attacks at companies and/or individuals.

- Whaling—Attacks targeting senior executives and stakeholders.

- Pharming—DNS cache poisoning to get user login credentials through a fake login landing page.

WHAT IS CYBER INSURANCE?

"Cyber" insurance is insurance coverage or policy that protects your practice from a cyberattack or a cyber threat. It provides coverage for liability claims involving the unauthorized release of information for which your practice may have the legal requirement to keep private or any claims alleging the invasion of privacy. It can also provide defense costs in state or federal regulatory proceedings that involve violations of privacy law. The term "cyber" implies coverage only for incidents that involve electronic hacking or online activities but can also provide coverage for other types of private data and communications in many different formats—paper, digital, or otherwise.

COMMON CYBER LIABILITY COVERAGES

IMPORTANT NOTE: Many practices think they have cyber liability insurance that will provide the types of broad protection outlined below as part of their business insurance policy when in fact they do not. These types of coverage are generally only found on specialized cyber insurance policies. If you don't carry $1 million of coverage at a minimum for cyber insurance, along with a broad list of coverage, you won't have enough to cover a cyber claim.

Privacy Liability (Including Employee Privacy)
The privacy liability unauthorized release of personally identifiable information (PII), protected health information (PHI), and corporate confidential information of third parties and employees.

Privacy Regulatory Claims Coverage
Privacy regulatory claims coverage provides coverage for both legal defense and the resulting fines and penalties coming from a regulatory claim that is alleging a privacy breach or a violation of a

federal, state, local, or foreign statute or regulation, with respect to privacy regulations.

Security Breach Response Coverage
This coverage reimburses you for costs you may have in the event of a security breach of personal, non-public information of your customers or employees. Examples of this type of expense can include the hiring of a public relations consultant for damage to your brand, IT forensics, customer notifications, and any potential first-party legal expenses to determine your obligations under applicable privacy regulations credit monitoring expenses for affected customers for up to twelve months or longer if required.

Security Liability Coverage
Protects against liability associated with your failure to prevent transmission of malicious code from their computer system to a third party's computer system.

Cyber Extortion Coverage
Covers expenses and payments (including ransom payments if necessary) to a third party to avert potential damage threatened, such as the introduction of malicious code, system interruption, data corruption or destruction, or dissemination of personal or confidential corporate information

Business Income and Digital Asset Restoration
The business income and digital asset restoration provides for lost earnings and expenses incurred because of a network disruption, or, an authorized third-party's inability to access a computer

system. It provides coverage for lost business as a result of a loss of reputation caused by any failure or disruption to computer systems. Restoration costs to restore or recreate digital (not hardware) assets to their pre-loss state are provided as well.

Cyber Deception Coverage

Cyber deception provides coverage for intentionally misleading you by means of a misrepresentation. Most often, it involves you transferring funds or providing personal information to a cybercriminal posing as a legitimate business or third party. This is commonly known as spear-phishing or social engineering.

Funds Transfer Fraud Coverage

Funds transfer fraud coverage provides coverage for unauthorized electronic funds transfer, theft of your money or other financial assets from your bank by electronic means, theft of your money or other financial assets from your corporate credit cards by electronic means, or any fraudulent manipulation of electronic documentation while stored on your computer systems.

Services Fraud Loss Coverage

Services fraud loss can cover "cryptojacking." There can be an increase in your computing resources because of cryptojacking, which can lead to excessive bandwidth charges you could unknowingly incur as a result of the incident.

Court Attendance Costs Coverage

Claims expenses and court-attendance costs provides you with reasonable expenses for attending court and other types of hearings in connection with a cyber event.

Post-Breach Response Coverage

Post-breach response provides you coverage for costs incurred for the completion of a network security audit, an information security risk assessment, and/or the implementation of security training.

Computer Hardware Coverage

Computer hardware coverage provides you with coverage to repair or replace any damaged, destroyed, or infected hardware associated with a cyberattack.

The list of coverages outlined above is by no means complete and every cyber liability policy is different. The current landscape for attacks, response, and coverage is evolving rapidly. Making sure you have front-end protection, monitoring, a response plan, and insurance to provide coverage in the event of a cyber-attack is critical.

ACTION ITEMS:

- Install email monitoring software.

- Use a secure VPN for all remote internet access.

- Create a cyber incident response plan.

- Review your cyber liability insurance on your current policy. If you don't have cyber insurance, **BUY IT NOW!** The average downtime for a business with a cyberattack is three weeks.

- Find an independent niche specialist that works with veterinary practices.

For insurance solutions that are best for your practice, contact me and I'll be happy to answer any questions you may have.

EMAIL: Bill@ButlerVetInsurance.com
PHONE 800-750-9775

Butler Vet Insurance

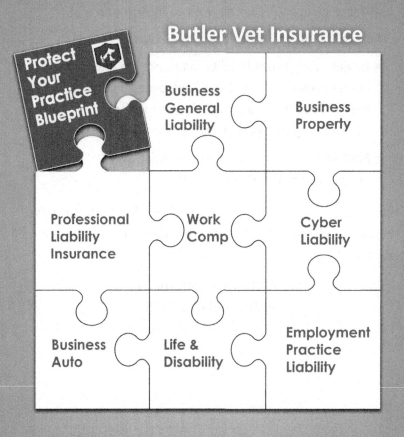

CHAPTER 8

LIFE / DISABILITY / BUSINESS OVERHEAD EXPENSE

This is a very deep topic all on its own so we will talk briefly about it here, in this book. Life and disability for veterinarians can encompass many different areas of the business from tax planning, practice perpetuation, income protection, and retirement. I will touch broadly on a number of ideas in this chapter that could be the starting point for a much deeper conversation with your insurance professional or financial advisor.

There is no one-size-fits-all plan when it comes to life or disability insurance for veterinarians, and the key question that needs to be answered when looking to place a policy is the following: "If this happens, what do we do now?" The goal is usually keeping the business alive either through perpetuation using a buy/sell agreement and life insurance or, if an owner or employee is disabled, then having the personal income or business revenue replaced.

Unfortunately, it is not uncommon that the best option is that if the owner of the practice dies, the practice is sold because there isn't a perpetuation plan in place. If a successor has not been identified within the practice who has the ability or desire to take over ownership and the ability to finance the purchase, selling is the only viable option. This is not something that most practice owners have not planned for in detail.

LIFE INSURANCE

There are many reasons to buy life insurance, and even more if you own a veterinary practice. The most common reasons you will purchase life insurance as the owner of the practice are burial-expenses payments, providing income replacement to your family, or because it may also be required by a lender or to fund a buy/sell agreement. Additionally, using life insurance as a financial investment strategy is another reason to explore life insurance. According to Chris Stefl, a managing partner at Versatile Insurance Services, a national life insurance broker, 5 percent to 10 percent of life insurance policies are used as part of a financial plan or investment strategy and the remaining 90 percent to 95 percent of the life-insurance policies sold are intended to provide a death benefit only. There are a number of different life insurance policies available and they generally fall into two different categories, term life insurance and permanent life insurance.

Term Life Insurance

Term life insurance is coverage for a defined period of time and death benefits, which is the amount the beneficiary will receive should the insured die during the policy term. It is generally less expensive and the underwriting and issue process is easier and faster. Some term life insurance policies may be converted to permanent insurance during the policy period or at the end of the policy term. These types of policies are most common and widely used at veterinary practices for buy/sell agreements, key person life policies, and to cover lender requirements.

Permanent Life Insurance

This type of life insurance covers you until death. These policies are more expensive and complicated than term life insurance as they can accrue interest, cash value, and will be with you as long as you pay the premiums all the way to the end of your life.

Depending on the type of permanent life policy you purchase, it may be part of your retirement strategy or be used to allow you, as the owner of the practice, to have access to liquid assets within the cash value of the life policy.

Common Types of Permanent Life Insurance

- Whole Life—Adds cash value during the "whole" life of the policy until death. The policy is in force until you stop paying premiums or death.

- Universal Life—Premiums are adjustable during the policy term as the cash value increases. You may take some of the cash value out of the policy or use it to pay the premiums.

- Variable Universal Life Insurance—This type of policy is a combination of whole and universal life insurance and adds the element of acting like a mutual fund in addition to the life insurance policy and savings account. You are in charge of where the cash value of your life insurance policy is invested.

- Indexed universal life insurance—This type of life insurance may be tied to the S&P 500, for instance, and if the market goes up, your insurance cash value does well, but if it goes down so does the cash value of the policy.

A couple of last items to note on permanent life policies. There are often fees associated with these policies that can, in some cases, be very large. You need to manage the policy like any other investment, you are adding to your cash value, premiums are paid to keep the policy current and it performs as intended.

Because of the complex nature of permanent life insurance and their higher cost, they are rarely used for the types of life policies needed to fund buy/sells, lender requirements, or income replacement for your family if you should die.

Recently, I was working with one of the practices we insure and they asked if I could assist them with some life insurance. One partner was selling their ownership share of the practice to an associate DVM that had been brought on board to help with the perpetuation of the practice. All three partners needed new life insurance policies as the oldest partner, age fifty-seven, had a policy that would be expiring in one year. The two younger partners, in their midthirties, needed new policies that would get them to retirement age. I was able to place twenty-five-year term life insurance policies for the two younger partners for roughly $110 a month, which will provide $1.3 million in death benefit to cover a buy/sell agreement. The older partner had a history of cancer, so his policy was more expensive and for a shorter term as he is closer to retirement age. He purchased a ten-year-old term policy for $750,000 of death benefit at $208 a month. To try and do this with permanent life insurance would have cost multiple thousands more a year, and would have taken oversight from management every year to make sure the policies were performing well.

Term insurance is easier, simpler, and less expensive than permanent insurance, which is why it is used over 90 percent to 95 percent of the time. There may be a place for permanent life insurance based on your needs, but it should be placed with a specific goal in mind and then managed along the way to achieve that goal.

Below are the main reasons needed to buy a life policy as a veterinarian who owns a practice:

Buy/Sell

If you bring on a partner and create a perpetuation plan for your practice, you will want to consult with a business attorney specializing in buy/sell agreements for veterinary practices. A buy/sell agreement is a legal agreement that lays out what happens to a business in the event of an owner or partner passing away. A buy/sell life policy pays the death benefit to fund the transition.

Key Person Life

This is life insurance on the owner of the practice or a "key person" within the practice. For example, if you have one associate DVM who generates 60 percent of your annual revenue or is a specialist, you can purchase a key person life policy on them. The practice will receive the death benefit in the event they die during their employment. The money can be used to replace the lost revenue they brought to the practice, assist in finding a replacement, and also pay hiring bonuses to their replacement.

Income Replacement

One of the most common issues with life insurance is that the family member who receives the death benefit from the life insurance does not do what is intended when you first purchased the policy. Often, life insurance is purchased to "pay off the house" or "put the kids through college" and a dollar amount is selected based on those needs. What happens in most cases is the death benefit gets put into the bank and spent over months or years to "replace" the lost income of the person who passed away.

EXAMPLE:
Veterinarian earns $125,000 annually
$450,000 Mortgage
$50,000 in Household Debt—Credit cards/ Auto Loans
$250,000 in Student Debt

In this example, the veterinarian may be advised to purchase $750,000 in life insurance death benefit to cover the "household" debt for their surviving spouse. The veterinarian dies and the surviving spouse deposits the $750,000 death benefit in the bank. The spouse then uses it to pay the normal monthly expenses over time to maintain the lifestyle that they were living prior to the death of the veterinarian. The problem is the money runs out in six years at $125,000 a year! After that, the surviving spouse can't afford to keep the house, cars, and lifestyle when the money runs out.

A better solution is to determine how long you want the surviving spouse to have the "income replaced" from the deceased veterinarian to maintain the lifestyle they enjoyed before the death of the policyholder. When working with our veterinarian clients, specifically the practice owner, we solve this issue by asking how long they would like their surviving spouse to have the same income coming in if they were no longer here, ten years, twenty years, or a lifetime? Using our carrier partners and a simple math formula, we purchase enough death benefit to replace the income for as long as it may be needed.

LENDER REQUIRED LIFE INSURANCE

When you purchase another practice, buy a building, or take out any kind of business loan your lender may require life insurance to cover the value of the loan. Start the life application process with enough time to have the policy in place to meet the closing date of the loan. Post-Covid, the time needed to underwrite life insurance has increased drastically due to the time it takes for medical providers to pull medical records if they are needed for underwriting a life policy. It is not uncommon for life insurance policy underwriting to exceed forty-five days if medical records are needed and should be accounted for when contemplating a large purchase where a loan may be required. **START EARLY!**

DISABILITY INSURANCE AND BUSINESS OVERHEAD EXPENSE

Both of these policies provide income replacement to the veterinarian or practice if you can't practice medicine.

Disability Insurance

This is a critical policy for all practice owners to have when the practice is smaller, just starting out, or you are the only veterinarian at the practice. Disability insurance usually provides a monthly benefit that is 60 percent of your normal income. This benefit would be paid to you personally so you or your family will not go without your income due to an injury that prevents you from being able to practice medicine as a veterinarian. When working with our veterinarian clients, there are some special considerations that we need to take into account. Some items on the policy that are unique to every veterinarian and should be considered are: Do you do surgeries? How long do you need to be disabled before you can collect the disability benefit? Can you consult and teach with a permanent disability? Are you able to do "any" occupation or your "own" occupation after injury and disability? These and more should be asked by any insurance specialist you do business with who will be able to advise you on the right disability policy for you to replace your lost income due to injury.

Business Overhead Expense

Business Overhead Expense insurance is a type of disability insurance that will pay a percentage of your business expenses in the event of disabling injury. As with disability insurance that replaces your household income, this insurance is a must for the smaller practice with only one or two key veterinarians who generate the majority of the revenue for the practice. When sold in combination, disability and business overhead expense provide a much-needed layer of business revenue protection for smaller practices. With disability insurance, you protect your personal income protection and with business overhead expense, your practice receives the policy benefit. In many cases, business overhead coverage may be required by your lender in addition to life insurance to protect the loan or financing.

As with life insurance policies, the underwriting time has stretched out from thirty days to close to ninety days or more for both disability and business overhead insurance, so plan ahead if you are looking to purchase either of these policies.

ACTION ITEMS:

- Review your current life insurance to make sure it will work as you intended.

- Purchase enough life insurance to replace your income and not just cover your household and final expenses.

- Get a quote for disability and business overhead expense.

- Find an independent insurance specialist that works with veterinary practices.

For insurance solutions that are best for your practice, contact me and I'll be happy to answer any questions you may have.

EMAIL: Bill@ButlerVetInsurance.com
PHONE 800-750-9775

CHAPTER 9

PROFESSIONAL LIABILITY INSURANCE

At this point, veterinary professional liability insurance is still reasonably priced. Because companion animals are valued as property, there are not large settlements or claim awards as seen in human medicine, but that may change in the future.

There are three main components to most veterinary professional liability policies: veterinary professional liability, license defense, and animal bailee coverage. These coverages can be purchased in two ways, as a stand-alone policy that each individual veterinarian at a practice would purchase or the practice may purchase for all of the associates. The other way to get coverage is to add it to your business insurance policy as an endorsement. The cost for each option is roughly the same and it depends on the practice and the DVMs working there on how they want to access this coverage.

VETERINARY PROFESSIONAL LIABILITY

Veterinary professional liability is standard medical malpractice insurance for a veterinarian and the rate charged by the carrier depends on the amount of coverage purchased and area of practice, companion, mixed, or large animal. For a veterinary practice that allows all of its associates to purchase their own coverage, it is important to set a minimum limit of coverage that each veterinarian must carry. This is important because veterinary professional liability policies cover the CVT, VTs, and staff working under the veterinarian for any medical malpractice claim. Many times, during a strategy session with the practice, there are a number of associate veterinarians at a practice with as little coverage as $100,000 and up to $3,000,000. A CVT working with a veterinarian in exam room one may have $100,000 in coverage and then go into exam room two with a different veterinarian and have $3,000,000 in coverage. It is critical to set a standard limit of required coverage that every associate veterinarian must carry so all the staff under your veterinarians are covered equally. If your practice purchases a stand-alone policy for each veterinarian, you can control the coverage, but if your associates buy the coverage themselves, you will want to see a copy of their policy on an annual basis to make sure they have the correct coverage you set as your practice minimums.

The other way veterinary professional liability insurance can be purchased is through the business insurance policy for the practice. The premium charged is based on the number of veterinarians that are on staff. Even if you have an associate that carries their own policy and your practice purchases this coverage through your business insurance, those associate veterinarians must be included in the headcount of veterinarians on staff.

LICENSE DEFENSE

I would consider this the most critical coverage as part of your veterinary professional liability policy. Because the value of the majority of animals seen by veterinarians in the United States is not very high, and you have a malpractice event your liability is low, all you owe is the actual cost to replace the animal. However, if the owner of that animal feels you were negligent and want to take things a step further or they are unsatisfied with only getting $500 for their dog or cat, they can lodge a complaint against you and refer you to the veterinary review board for your state. Having insurance to defend your license is critical to make sure that you are able to continue to practice medicine. Depending on the policy, you can purchase $100,000 of license defense coverage at this time, about $100 a year. Don't skip this important coverage.

ANIMAL BAILEE

Bailee is an old insurance term that refers to coverage for others' property while it is in your "care, custody, or control." For veterinarians and your practices, these are your patients. Depending on the scope of your practice, you want to purchase enough coverage in the event of catastrophic loss of all the animals under your care at one time or the highest valued animal you may see. This coverage is inexpensive in relation to all the other coverages purchased and adding a little extra is a good idea. Buying enough coverage for the worst that can happen should be the goal, especially with inexpensive coverages like license defense and animal bailee.

In many cases, I have seen the practices I work with being double covered by veterinary professional liability insurance. The agent or agency you use may not understand that you purchase veterinary professional liability insurance as a stand-alone insurance policy through national associations and add the coverage onto the business insurance policy you have. This can add hundreds or thousands of premium dollars to your policy depending on the size of your practice, and you may overpay for years because the agent doesn't understand your practice.

ACTION ITEMS:

- Make sure all veterinarians at your practice carry the same level of coverage.

- Add license defense and animal bailee coverage.

- If you and your associates purchase veterinary professional liability as a stand-alone policy, confirm it is not endorsed onto your business insurance policy and you have double coverage.

- Find an independent niche specialist that works with veterinary practices.

For insurance solutions that are best for your practice, contact me and I'll be happy to answer any questions you may have.

EMAIL: Bill@ButlerVetInsurance.com
PHONE 800-750-9775

ACKNOWLEDGMENTS

This book would not have been possible without the support of my wife, Shannon. She has been there for me when I needed her most and never wavered in her support of me or my work. I am so grateful to have her as my partner, wife, and best friend. I'm a lucky guy!

A special thanks goes to my parents, Dan and Linda, who have had belief and faith in me my whole life. The unconditional love was sometimes tough love and has been the foundation of everything I have been able to accomplish in life, this book included. I learned how to network and what hard work meant from my dad. He was never afraid to try anything and I am so fortunate he always believed in me. From my mom, I learned it's never too late to try something new in life. As a lifelong learner, she has always had a thirst for knowledge and I have implemented that in my own life. Thanks, Mom and Dad.

I was invited to a coaching boot camp in the fall of 2014 by Jerry Hendrickson and was introduced to my business coach, friend, and mentor Mike Stromsoe. Both Jerry and Mike have had a huge, positive impact on me, both personally and professionally. I will be eternally grateful to Jerry for suggesting I attend that first coaching boot camp and Mike for sharing his wisdom, mentorship, and friendship over the years.

Mike's coaching program has allowed me to network with some of the best and brightest in the insurance industry. My Unstoppable

Profit Producer family, Nancy Mendazibal, David Brush Jose and Karla Soriano, Allison Finney, Todd Payne, Connie Baumann (thanks for cookies), Lorin Zitting, Ben Walker, Ginny Buchanan, and Mandy Smith. Big shout out to the UPP team, Andrea Wyatt and Joel Mckinley. Thank you for always being there for me when I need you all the most. #AMFF.

The following authors, agents, friends, and family have had a huge impact on me in my life. George **W.** Pearce, Oliver **H**. Butler, Tom Butler, the McGuires, Dan Riley, April Goodin, Patty Lares, Chris Paradiso, Claudia McClain, Bob Klinger, Scott Howell, Russ Castle, Jesse Parenti, Kevin Stiener, Kelly Tighe, Frank Whitcomb, agents and agencies of the NIAA, Joe Theismann, Rudy Ruettiger, Kevin Eastman, Russell Brunson, Jim Collins, Brené Brown, Jeb Blount, Malcolm Gladwell, Donna Kimmes, David Goggins, Ranger Class 02-00 Classmates & Ranger Instructors, SSG White, Sean Staum, Phil Defibo, Jason Stamer, Tony Padilla, Chad Malmberg, Mike Lubovitch, Mike Nielson, Matt Aschelman, Deirdre Van Nest, and of course many more.

My fellow Rotarians in the Rotary Club of Apple Valley, Minnesota.

An extra note of gratitude and thanks to the team at Butler & Associates Insurance Agency and Butler Vet Insurance for helping us do what we do.

Last, I want to thank James Malinchak. In 2015, James was the featured guest on a webinar, and, during the Q&A at the end, I was able to ask him what was the number one thing I should be doing or investing in as an entrepreneur. He said that the best investment I could make was in myself and I should hire a business coach. It has been the best business decision I have ever made and set in motion a chain of events over the past eight years that has led to massive personal and professional success. This book is part of that chain of events. Thank you, James.

GLOSSARY

Animal Bailee: Coverage for animals in your care, custody, or control if they are injured or killed.

BAP: Business Auto Policy

BOP: Business Owners Insurance Policy

Business Personal Property: Practice property-like equipment; x-ray, pet food inventory.

Business Overhead Expense: Business revenue protection in the event you become disabled.

CGL: Commercial General Liability Insurance

CPP: Commercial Package Policy

Cyber Incident: A security event that compromises the integrity, confidentiality, or availability of an information asset.

Cyber Breach: An incident that results in the confirmed disclosure— not just potential exposure—of data to an unauthorized party.

Death Benefit: Payout amount on a life insurance policy.

Disability Insurance: Income replacement for short- or long-term disability.

Deductible: Your share of a claim represented in a dollar amount or percent of claim and or coverage.

EPLI: Employment Practice Liability Insurance

Experience: Payroll and claims over a given time period.

Experience Modification: Calculation of your claims and payroll data for a given amount of time, can add or reduce the premium on workers' compensation insurance.

Endorsement: Additional coverage added to a property and casualty insurance.

Frequency: Number of claims in a given period of time.

Hired Auto: Coverage for vehicles rented to the practice.

Inland Marine: Coverage for high-value equipment or equipment that leaves your practice for off-site visits.

Non-Owned Auto: Coverage for your practice if employees use their personal vehicles in the course of business.

Rate of Remuneration: Premium charged per $100 of estimated payroll on workers' compensation insurance.

Reserve: Estimated cost of a given claim.

Remuneration: Payroll reported on workers' compensation insurance.

Rider: Additional coverage added to a life, health and, disability insurance.

Severity: Amount of claim or claims paid.

Self-Insured Retention: See deductible.

Term Life Insurance: Life insurance sold for a set death benefit, set amount of time, and premium.

Whole Life Insurance: Life insurance policy that pays a death benefit and also accumulates cash value.

Universal Life Insurance: Flexible life insurance policy that pays a death benefit, accumulates cash value, and has adjustable premiums.

BIBLIOGRAPHY

1. IIABA. 2021. *Big I Market Share Report 2021.*

2. Insurance Services Office. 2013. *Business Auto Coverage Form (CA 00 01 10 13).*

3. TrustedChoice.com. 2021. "How Employment Practices Liability Insurance Has Your Back." https://www.trustedchoice.com/business-insurance/liability/epli/.

4. IBM Security, ed. 2022. Cost of a Data Breach Report 2022.

MOTIVATE AND INSPIRE OTHERS!

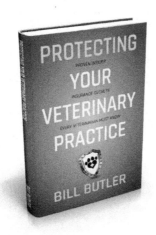

"Share This Book"
Retail $15.97

5–20 Books	$13.97
21–99 Books	$11.97
100–499 Books	$9.97
500–999 Books	$7.97
1,000+ Books	$5.97

TO PLACE AN ORDER CONTACT:

Butler Vet Insurance
Po Box 240326
Apple Valley MN 55124

Direct / Text 952-208-7220
Toll Free 800-750-9775

www.ButlerVetBook.com/Order

THE IDEAL PROFESSIONAL SPEAKER FOR YOUR NEXT EVENT!

Any organization that wants to educate their people on insider insurance secrets for Veterinary Practices needs to hire Bill Butler for a keynote and/or workshop training!

TO CONTACT OR BOOK BILL TO SPEAK:

Butler Vet Insurance
Po Box 240326
Apple Valley MN 55124

Direct / Text 952-208-7220
Toll Free 800-750-9775

www.billbutlerspeaker.com

THE IDEAL INSURANCE AGENT FOR YOU!

If you're ready to work with an agency and insurance professional that understands you and your industry you will love having Bill as your Agent!

TO CONTACT BILL BUTLER CIC, CISR, CWCA:

Butler Vet Insurance
Po Box 240326
Apple Valley MN 55124

Direct / Text 952-208-7220
Toll Free 800-750-9775

www.ButlerVetInsurance.com

BILL BUTLER'S

PROTECTING YOUR VETERINARY PRACTICE

Insider Insurance Secrets Every Veterinarian Must Know!

Special **<u>FREE</u>** Bonus Gifts for You!!!

To help you Protect Your

Practice, there are

FREE BONUS RESOURCES

for you at:

www.ButlerVetBook.com

ABOUT THE AUTHOR

Bill Butler is originally from Wisconsin and is the only child of Dan and Linda Butler. He moved with his family to Minnesota in 1986 and now resides in Burnsville, Minnesota, with his wife, Shannon and their cat, Louie. He enlisted into the infantry with the Minnesota Army National Guard in 1993, and during his twelve-year career with the army, served in various units within the Minnesota Army National Guard and 101st Airborne Division.

Since joining his parents at their insurance agency in Apple Valley in 2004, Bill has worked in all areas of the agency, from service and sales to agency operations, and was named president of the agency in 2017, which is the same year he founded Butler Vet Insurance. Butler Vet Insurance is the niche commercial division at Butler & Associates Insurance Agency dedicated to helping veterinarians protect everything they have worked so hard for. Understanding the importance of being able to educate his clients, Bill has focused on educating himself within the industry and has earned the following designations: certified insurance service representative, certified insurance counselor, and certified work comp advisor.

Butler & Associates Insurance Agency has been recognized nationally within the insurance industry as a top agency and was named Rough Notes Agency of the Month in July 2019. Rough Notes serves the insurance industry and has been in publication since 1878.

He has been a member of the Minnesota Independent Agents and Brokers Association, MIABA, since starting his insurance career in 2004. Bill was named Minnesota Young Agent of the Year in 2012 and is currently a director at large for the Minnesota Independent Agents and Brokers Association.

Bill is active in his local community as the president-elect for the Rotary Club of Apple Valley, Foundation Secretary for the Apple Valley Rotary Scholarship Foundation and is passionate about giving back to others locally, regionally, and globally through Rotary projects and grants.

Leading his team, protecting his clients, and working to build a "GREAT" business are what drives Bill to take action every day.

Bill Butler is president of Butler & Associates Insurance Agency Inc. and founder of Butler Vet Insurance, focusing on insurance for the veterinary and pet services industry. He spent twelve years in the military with the Minnesota Army National Guard and US Army, serving in various roles both in Minnesota and 101st Airborne Division, Ft. Campbell, Kentucky, before entering the insurance industry. He is active in his local business community, veterinary associations, and Rotary Club, and is passionate about giving back to others. Originally from Milwaukee, Wisconsin, he and his wife, Shannon, reside in Burnsville, Minnesota.

www.butlerveterinarybook.com
www.butlervetinsurance.com

Cover Design and Layout: Dawn Teagarden
Author Photographs: Val Westover

Made in the USA
Columbia, SC
30 November 2024

48036149R00078